FAIR TO PIDDLING

A JOURNEY THROUGH MIDLIFE IN HUMOROUS VERSE

BY LIZZIE NELSON

Lisa Nelson

Fair to Piddling

ISBN (Print Edition): 978-1-54399-219-9

ISBN (eBook Edition): 978-1-54399-220-5

For my mother.

CONTENTS

INTRODUCTION

Do you find yourself saying, "Stop me if I've told you this before"? Or, "I can't eat that, it'll go right through me!" Or even, "Hang on, I just need another quick pee." And especially, "What was I just saying?" Then, hello there! We are fellow travelers.

What seemed like a particularly swift journey for me—from the bubbling springs of youth to the estuary of middle age—was actually the happiest. Although it felt shortened by an early menopause, it was made more than tolerable by a sense of humor and a loving family. I recognize my good fortune in my family; it is what I wanted. I also recognize that for some women, it didn't happen or was simply not a requirement. I hope this book still resonates here and there for all women, and that above all, it raises a smile.

We need to laugh because ageing might seem a little discouraging, and yet our lines should be read as love and laughter shared. Our little aches and twinges are mementos from our journeys, our bellies tell of children or the food and drink that delighted us, and the gray hairs grow for our battles fought and worries wrought. We are full of stories, inside and out. Middle age is when we are absolutely ready to share our wisdom and experience. Ageing brings a realization of worth and as a woman in my fifties I feel purposeful, beautiful and recognize my equality and validity in every single space because in midlife, do we know everything? Yes, we bloody well do! We just can't always bring it to mind immediately.

These poems are inspired by events and conversations from my own journey, from parenthood and a simultaneous perimenopause to post-menopause. I talk a great deal with my mother, who, although diminished in height, still grows in wit and wisdom. We talk a little about the inevitable, and we do so with levity. And that's OK. I swear just a tiny bit in this book, and that is me, so that's OK too. You may also notice a muddle of Anglo-American spelling and phrases. After thirteen years of living in the States, I have become somewhat of a blend of cultures and this book simply reflects who I am.

This collection is also for those who share our lives and love us. It may help you understand our inner struggles, like that fuzzy cotton-headed feeling, empty yet completely full of fluff, and our battles with those unwelcome physical changes. We often feel only fair to middling. Or lately and often unexpectedly, fair to piddling.

THIRTIES:
LITTLE PEOPLE

FOOD DIARY

*(Or My Favorite Things —With Apologies to
The Sound of Music and Julie Andrews)*

Day 1

Honey on oatmeal and walnuts and apple.

Warm chicken salad and a small toasted bagel.

Brown rice-stuffed lettuce leaves
bundled with chive.

Turkey breast curry with curly endive.

Day 2

Berries on melon and crispy rice cereal.

Blob of Greek yogurt, three tiny falafels.

Big bunch of celery with cottage cheese.

Two handfuls of M&M's and a Chinese!

Day 3

Fat-free egg muffin and full-fat soy latte.

Carrots and radishes, a little biscotti.

Bacon- and cheese-loaded potato skins.

Some glasses of wine, diet tonic and gin!

Day 4

Scrambled egg whites.

Pecan pie slice.

Pack of stringy cheese.

A small bag of nuts and a bowlful of chips,

three helpings of Bolognese!

Day 5

Pancakes and muffins with syrup and butter.

Leftover pasta I was saving for supper.

A tiny bowl of vanilla ice cream,

pizza and garlic bread, (quite) a few jelly beans.

Sticking to this sodding diet

makes me feel so sad,

but I look in the fridge and my favorite things

look back saying, "Yes! Be bad!"

Handbags 30's to 50's

That 'Remember When
You Were Out Every Night
& Only Needed a Lipstick Bag'

Then the 'Bare Essentials
for the Baby' Bag

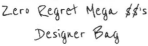

Dear God! A Date Night!
Babysitter Phoning Bag

Zero Regret Mega $$'s
Designer Bag

What-the-Hell-Was-I-Thinking
-in-a-Menopausal-Fog Bag

HANDBAG

At the bottom of my bag

live the things that I need,

like old shopping lists and

wee mystery keys.

Chocolate fragments

white bloomed,

coupons past good,

pennies by the dozen,

and pills that could

have been meant

for the dogs or kids, but hey!

Until one gets sick,

that's where they'll stay.

The bottom of my bag,

I fear one day,

will get me pulled up

by the TSA.

But what drives me crazy

is digging around

for the stuff you really need

that can never be found,

like a pen or tissue

or stamps or a quarter

that should be down there,

but never when they oughta!

At the bottom of my bag

is the end to this verse,

scribbled on a scrap

in the depths

of my purse.

THANKS, KIDS!

Droopy tits

Saggy bits

Belly hides your toes

Hands of leather

Nails that will never

Be nice to paint and grow

Hairs that spring

From everything

And careful when you sneeze;

Things aren't as tight

But this just might

Be the best thing

I ever did.

NANO NANNY

(My Shrinking Granny)

My nanny's got so tiny

that when we have her here for tea,

we make her mini muffins

and feed her on my knee.

I love my nanny dreadfully

so I'm careful where I tread,

and when it gets to seven o'clock,

she helps with bath and bed.

I scoop her up and put her in
my favorite wind-up sub,

and she sails around me in my bath

and tells me where to scrub!

But I'm not allowed to have bubbly stuff

because the other day

she got sucked inside a bubble,

and floated clean away!

When it's time for bed

she reads me books, though
it can be hard to hear,

so I pick her up on a cotton-wool bud

and sit her on my ear!

She may come around at breakfast,

it helps my mum to cope,

though it's always tricky to set up

the electron microscope!

You may have noticed, since you started

this verse from the very top,

that my nanny's been shrinking all the while

and now lives

in this

full stop

.

IT'S NOT THE END OF THE WORLD

"What day is it today, Mummy?"

I look at you in the rearview mirror.

We're almost at school.

"It's Tuesday, Love. Why?"

"Nooooooo!

Stop the car! Stop the car!

We have to go back home!"

Big tears roll down crimson cheeks.

"What on Earth is the matter?

Don't upset yourself,

nothing can be that bad."

"My knickers say 'Friday,'

they have 'Friday' written on them!"

I pull over.

This is bad.

"What about your socks?

What do they say?"

Gulping back sobs,

I hear the dreadful words

that reduce this sunny day

into tummy-turning HORROR!

"Well . . . one says, it says . . .

'Monday'

and the other, *sniff*

says . . .

'THURSDAY!'"

The world around us

starts to wobble

as the universe

struggles to heal

this rift in the space-time continuum.

Asockalypse!

LET'S HAVE A VIDEO CHAT!

You're all there

and we're all here,

then let us call you.

Yes! Won't that be lovely?

We can hear you,

but you're very pixilated.

That's better.

Maybe not.

Well this is nice.

Oh, can't you see us? Our camera is on.

Let me fiddle with it.

Here we are,

now you've gone.

How about now?

Great. Isn't this nice!

Yes, you're still very fuzzy

and it keeps freezing.

No news, no . . .

well I only spoke to you last week.

You all look well.

Are those new curtains?

Oh! Guess they just look different.

This is great, though, isn't it?

You've completely frozen, again.

Are the kids still awake?

Hello, Sweetheart!

You in your pajamas already?

Yes, she's here, she'd love to see you!

She'd love to tell you about her new bike.

No, I don't think we want to see your bottom,

no! Don't encourage her! Kids, please!

Good.

Now isn't this lovely!

We should do this more often.

MOM-ENTARY ENVY

We lie together side by side

on my pluffy bed;

your lovely little knocky knees,

my big pink Mummy legs.

Your big toes turn in perfect circles

and I try to do it too,

but I'm no longer agile

and rubbery like you.

I watch you fold yourself in half,

your feet behind your head

and roll, a ball of giggles,

contorting round the bed.

And for a moment, I recall

how it was to be so supple,

to fall without falling hard

and be all mirth and muscle.

To wear Band-Aids just like medals

from wars with bikes and grit,

when you only cried a little,

then cleaned your wounds with spit.

No breasts that weigh,

no bones that ache,

no injuries that linger.

You wept less from bloody grazes

and more for just a splinter.

I draw you in to squeeze you tight

and smell your apple scent;

you are bright like spring and summer,

and that's nothing I resent.

You restore what years have stolen

and I feel vicariously renewed;

I may not be up to somersaults,

but I'll always play with you.

DECEPTIONS OF
AN EVERYTHING'S
YUMMY MUMMY

That chocolate rabbit the Easter Bunny gave you?

You did nibble the ears off, gosh!
Don't you remember?

Oh! Those scrummy little caramel
desserts I got for your lunch box?

Yes, they only come in packs of three; that
space in the box is for the cool air to circulate.

I'm glad you liked those crispy, roast potatoes.

No, sorry, there were no golden crunchy
chibbly bits left in the pan.

You silly moo! We only bought one tub of
gourmet organic ice cream at the farm shop!

That sign didn't say "Buy One Get One Free,"
it said, "Buy One and the Goat Goes Free!"

No, I don't think there's meant to
be a big chocolate in your advent
calendar for the twenty-fourth,

the empty space is to remind you of Jesus's
lowly birth; poverty, sacrifice, and all that.

Yes, Dear, it makes me feel sad too.

There was a recall for all the
coconut licorice allsorts.

I had to mail them back to the factory for testing.

And all the other allsorts they touched.

Um, those are not rainbow
sprinkles round my mouth.

It's my new lipstick, actually!

Drinking 30's to 50's

Obviously, This Was
a Great Night Out

So Embarrassing... Ok
Let's Order Another

Smoothie?

New Me

Sod That, It's err..Monday!

A Nice Cuppa Tea

CRAVING

Watching telly as my mind scans the kitchen.

Damn that post dinner sweet choccy itchin'.

Probing shelves but all are bare.

There is her Easter choc but don't think I dare.

Takes a will of iron not to break that trust

between mother and child

but fuck it,

needs must.

FREE SAMPLING AT COSTCO

Jelly Bean Lady, hooray! Our favorite!

But as we reach your stand

we find we were mistaken.

Tis only the Vitamin Powder Lady.

I should have known,

with no one hovering around you;

you are an island

in the stream

and they flood past,

not catching your eye.

I sense your sorrow

but we do not stop to sample.

Perhaps tomorrow

they'll give you

a less shit job.

IN (AND OUT) PARENTHESIS

I'm a good mum

(although, sometimes, she
watches too much TV)

I love to play with her

(but I feel rotten when I start thinking
I need to be doing something else)

I worry about her nutrition

(although she had pizza twice this weekend)

I watch her perform and am so proud

(I don't think her fearlessness came from me)

I tell her off for being sneaky,
swiping another cookie

(she totally got that from me)

I have to ask her to do stuff umpteen times

(I am inherently lazy)

seeing her upset breaks my heart

(but wiping away her tears brings me joy)

I love her

(I love her)

FORTIES: CHANGES

POSSIBLY STILL GOOD
FOR A STIR FRY

Some mornings

I look at my face

and feel a pang of loss.

Like a thing once

fresh and succulent,

forgotten then found,

grayed and desiccated

and stuck to the back

of the fridge.

I exaggerate.

Yet I am too old to be salad.

LEAVING THE HOUSE

Cooker off; check!

Windows shut; check!

Iron off; check!

Everything unplugged; check!

Back door locked; rattle, rattle; check!

Cooker off; double check!

Alarm on, out the door, lock the door,

check I locked the door; rattle, rattle; check!

Unlock the door,

check I put the alarm on,

lock the door,

check it's locked.

Get in car,

run back, check the door.

(You think I'm joking.)

Drive away with horrible nagging sensation

that I only imagined it

and didn't actually

check the cooker.

And as I go down the hill,

I pass, going the other way,

all lights and sirens,

a fire engine.

Fuck.

LET'S FACE IT

I've got creams for brightening, tightening,

peeling and plumping,

wrinkles and crinkles,

and lifting and sculpting.

For filling and firming,

regrading, refining,

restoring, repairing,

renewing, rewinding.

There's resurfacing scrub you could
use on some pavements,

a stingly astringent and fragrance-free fragrance.

There are big frosted jars bought
at terrible expense;

open and find just a thimble of contents!

There's stuff for defending, fighting, protecting,

resisting, reviving, and I suspect, resurrecting!

But for all the stuff I have got for my face,

you'd assume I look marvelous, glowing, just ace!

But there is no reduction of
fine lines and wrinkles;

I still have those crow's feet

and dark spots and sprinkles.

I doubt I'll give in, I'll keep trying these things.

This not-so-spring chicken

to spring vainly clings.

Face Creams 30's to 50's

Imaginary Fine Lines
& Age Spot Cream $20

Losing Elasticity
All Downhill Now $45

Placental Stem Cell
Serum $120

Illuminating Butter
With Nasty
Bits of Glitter $75

100,000 Mile Service
& Oil Change $150

Actual Nano
Plastic Surgeons $750

BEARDS

Even men who were just OK are hot;

why can't I have what they have got?

If I could grow a beard, you see,

I could stroke it when in reverie.

I could tuck a little chocolate in,

then magic it from neath my chin.

I could color it to complement

my favorite lipstick or ornament.

I could weave it, bead it, make it feathery,

or trim it just like topiary!

You see, I'm jealous, truth be told;

men are favored in this world.

But it's so unfair and I call foul!

Because I need one

to hide my jowls!

TOENAILS

Squinting to clip them,
I put on reading glasses
But can't get my foot
Up close enough to focus.
This is middle age, this is.

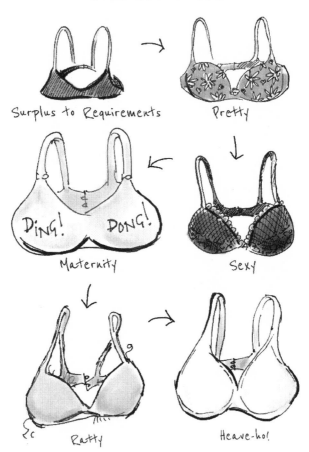

Bras 30's to 50's

Surplus to Requirements

Pretty

Maternity

DING! DONG!

Sexy

Ratty

Heave-ho!

BRA

Oh, sweet liberty!

That point in the evening

when you unclip and

magic it out of your sleeve.

Release the tatas. Tada!

MY THONG SONG

Feeling like only

yethterday

I wore

that thong

and felt all thexy.

I never thought ahead

back then for long

on how aging

would affect me.

But my tiny thong,

that yethterday

hath now become tomorrow,

and tho I throw you in the bin

with a little thong of thorrow.

NEVER TO BE SAID TO HER

We used to be so sweet,

sleeping nose to nose,

and though we're getting older,

our affection only grows.

So it was no surprise the other day

when you reached out to brush my face

and I looked up adoringly,

oozing loveliness and grace.

The words that I anticipated,

that love, over time, allows,

were not what came from twixt your lips:

"You've got some crumbs stuck to your jowls."

HOT LOVE

I love you through all of your flashes and flares,

and when you forget where you're
going at the top of the stairs.

Your ups and your downs in
your cotton-wool head;

I love you when blue,

I love you bright red.

On a cold wintry night

it has to be said,

O Menopausal Woman,

come warm up my bed!

INSOMNIAAAARGH!

*(Or, Never Turn On Your Phone
in the Middle of the Night)*

3:00 a.m. Hot.

I open my eyes a little bit

and reach for my phone.

Stupid thing to do.

Pained by the light,

my eyes wake up

and scan the news.

Terrible things.

Terrible things

and Kim Kardashian.

I read about her and her bum.

I don't want to;

reason hasn't kicked in yet.

I read about politicians

and world leaders.

Some bad people

doing heinous things.

Makes me angry.

I read about another Kardashian

and another

and another.

They make me feel

absolutely nothing.

So that's OK.

I should try to sleep,

maybe counting

Kardashians . . .

but not sure who's who.

I look at the news.

Terrorists.

Evil.

Bleak.

And puppies!

Puppies best friends with tiger cubs

and baby pandas;

I'm watching roly-poly baby pandas

and little orphan orangutans.

I could sleep now.

Where are their mothers?

What happened?

Something bad I bet.

Bad world.

Snoring, he's snoring.

That and the Kardashians:

really annoying!

He's stopped, he's holding his breath.

Lose weight, I should lose weight.

This new diet looks good.

I'll look at the meal planner.

Oh, my God!

Who can be arsed to buy and cook

all that stuff?

Too complicated,

too expensive.

That person has never had to diet,

her bum has always looked like that.

That's a model, not a real . . .

He still hasn't breathed.

That's like sleep apnea, isn't it?

I should look that up.

That's a long time for not breathing.

I should poke him.

But then he might start snoring again.

I should look up how to resuscitate someone.

Wow! That looks hard.

I'll leave it.

If the worst happens,

I can always say I was asleep.

I'm so tired,

so very tired.

PERIOD DRAMA

I love period dramas,

I watch them all;

those tales of the poxed and the beautiful,

the lush landscapes, the costumes,

the lovelorn and lusty.

I eat up every candlelit ballroom

and every field in harvest.

Each well-appointed townhouse

to every dusty hayloft.

I love the highborn in billowing silks and velvet,

and the sweaty laborer in open-necked muslin.

I love the children in their pantaloons,

I love the grubby urchins.

I want flowers in my hair

and God-knows-what on my shoes.

I am born out of time.

I am a girl of Melstock, of Casterbridge.

I am a Warleggan. No! I'm a Poldark:

I am twenty years younger and ride
sidesaddle, like it's nothing,

along the cliffs

until my horse bolts

and I'm helpless.

But here comes Tom Hiddleston,

back from the wars, in uniform,

thundering toward me on his
enormous black stallion.

And he pulls me onto his beast

and I am indignant

and all crushed up against him.

I struggle a teensy bit.

I say, "Where's Bess?
Get my bloody horse!"

And he is shocked but intrigued

and even a little amused by my bad language.

"You're a feisty one!" says he,

and he's right; I'm unlike anyone he's ever met

because I'm actually from 1989.

And I open my eyes

and look up at my husband

and wonder where his mutton
chops and brass buttons went

and why he isn't Tom Hiddleston.

He brushes the stray curls from my face

and the dribble from my cheek

and tells me I was snoring, so he
turned over to *Top Gear*.

And I'm back in the present.

And it's all right.

Kind of.

OLD SPICE

My cardamom is in a jar in my spice drawer.

I remember buying it.

I know I have some.

Little green pods.

Ah, but here they are . . .

and not so green anymore.

It wasn't so long ago, was it?

She was still little,

we were trying different things.

We bought this nutmeg

for a dish

for a school potluck.

Cloves for Christmases,

almost empty.

Here's my star anise and

cinnamon, no fragrance left.

Do things not last?

Or has that much time really passed?

She is all grown up.

I wish I had stopped to savor

every ounce

and make the most

of my most precious commodity.

FIFTIES:
FORGETFULNESS

CLIMBING THE STAIRS

The crunching, scrunching

of grinding shards,

like a liquidizer turning

grit. A witch's cauldron

filled with jelly and bones

churning around in it.

Like waves pulling

pebbles, clicking and scraping,

as they're forced to roll back to the

sea. The crack and spit

of a roaring fire pit:

these are all the sounds

of my knees!

Shoes 30's to 50's

Those Shoes You Wore
to Everyone's Wedding

Fun Mum!

Thank You, Santa

Wicked Toe Bleeding
Party Boots

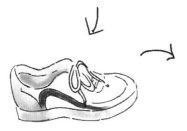

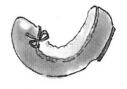

I'm Still Trendy
(& a Bit Sporty)

'Flat' Shoes

MATURE TV

My dinner's getting cold.

Why does it take so long to find

the bit we got to

in that new thriller

where we both fell asleep

the night before?

Can you hear that?

That's better.

What's that letter he's holding up,

what does it say?

Pause it and I'll get up close and read it.

Oh look, it's her! What's-her-name!

She was in that other thingy.

God! She's looking craggy.

How old do you think she is?

Oh.

I'm lost. Who's that guy?

I've got no bloody idea what's going on.

You know what's going on?

Was I asleep?

I wasn't asleep!

What happened?

Oh! It's a flashback.

Ugh! Sex scenes! Can we fast forward?

You done? No, I don't think
we've got any chocolate.

I don't know what happened to
that bar from last night.

Maybe the dog got hold of it.

Yes, I ate it.

Want to do the next episode?

It's nine thirty.

Yes, let's live a little.

What happened?

I was out cold.

DESTINATION

Menopause is a journey with no map.

You must write down where you're going

all the time or you'll forget why you're there

or here or wherever.

Try to remember what you wrote it on

and where you put it.

I say, always put it back

in the same place you found it,

even if it is a silly place.

I say, it may even be worth making a note

of that place and putting that

somewhere sensible

or silly.

But then again . . .

Menopause is a journey through time, not space.

An interdimensional, alternate universe,

out-of-body odyssey.

There will be times when you
are not in the same room

as your physical self.

And someone is talking to you

but there isn't enough of you in you

to comprehend.

Because you're mostly floating on the ceiling.

I say,

there isn't an awful lot you can do

about that.

QUEST

What am I here for?

I no longer know.

My purpose has fled,

my intent in shadow,

cast by the light

that enlightens me not;

I stand alone,

devoid of all thought.

The chill of winter

fingers my face.

My future seems frozen.

My past can't be retraced.

What am I here for?

Am I lost evermore?

I step back, defeated,

and close the fridge door.

MAP

Here, on my hand, where a lino cutter missed.

Here, on my toe, where I pinned myself
to the lawn with a garden fork.

Here, on my elbow, from when I
ran by a pool and slipped.

Don't admire my many scars like I'm
some old warrior because mostly,

I've been a complete tit.

Knickers 30's to 50's

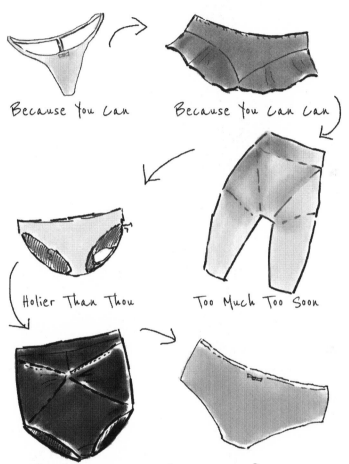

Because You Can

Because You Can Can)

Holier Than Thou

Too Much Too Soon

The New Sexy.
Yes it is, Actually!

Horriblest Color from Multi-pack
(Pray You Don't End Up
n the ER Today)

BIG KNICKERS

Big knickers, big knickers,

up to my waist!

I love you, big knickers,

my bum's fully encased.

I encourage you all,

make the change, liberate;

scrap the flimsy and itchy

that gets swallowed behind;

go for some volume,

not a sexy design.

You'll get marble-cold cheeks

in French knickers of satin,

and you can't survive

in shapewear that flattens.

Seamless takes minutes to

fall down to your knees

and lacey ensures

that your fanny will freeze.

You'll only trap farts

in spandex and nylon,

it's not rocket science

that you're better in cotton.

I'm just saying, be kind

and pamper your bottom.

COTTON WOOL HEAD

What stuff is this cotton wool behind my eyes?

A knit of foggy fibers holding
fast my next thought.

Odd when my mind so flies and at
the age of fifty-three I ought

to relish this ripe wisdom and cognition.

Yet here I am, forgetting where to turn

just to reach the kitchen.

HAIRS

There are too few left

around my foo foo,

but there are four more on my nose.

Mother Nature has her reasons,

but buggered if I knows.

DOG YEARS

Sometimes, I feel old;

little twinges and back spasms.

I catch a reflection that hints at

the face I will own in my dotage.

In dog years, I am already old.

I am an old, stiff, farty dog

that can't be arsed to fetch a stick

or nothin'.

That growls when she doesn't
want to be disturbed

and snaps at careless youngsters.

That has twitchy dreams

of flying through hayfields

and meeting silky strangers

that share her basket,

but who always turn out to be

that warm familiar mate she will always love.

I am this dog,

not so young, not so fit,

who still enjoys her food

and a nice fondle.

EXPIRY DATE

When I am old,

I bet I'll be found

starved to death,

in bed,

surrounded by

a hundred cartons of food

I could not bloody open.

The "easy open" kind.

Or else discovered choked:

choked

and desiccated

by the little

sachet of silica

that I thought was

seasoning

for my veggie chips.

Asphyxiated

as the air

in my lavatory

was replaced by clouds

of alpine meadow mist;

the fragrant fart from

a thoughtfully sculpted yet

fugly piece of plastic

sat atop my loo.

Poached

inside out

because of the failing seal

on my microwave door.

But in any case, I knew

I should have left the house

every time I turned it on

(and even put a good

half mile between me

and it).

Preserved.

Found mummified,

wrapped in clothing

from my tumble dryer

that was softened by little sheets

suffused with

formaldehyde.

But was blissfully unaware

because, handily,

they also contained

chloroform.

Or simply found chock-full

of tiny blue polyurethane balls

that were in my toothpaste

all these years.

Expired.

Conspired against

for living a life

of convenience.

VIKING FUNERAL

On getting older and planning my funeral
I have a particular wish:
to float out on a boat like a Viking,
a spectacular kind of finish.

Pile me high with my every possession,
set light, push me off when you're done;
I'll float out incandescent and blazing
to meet and to melt with the sun.

I don't want it all to go tits up,
so plan well, and before you begin
check weather, wind speed, and direction,
and if the tide's outward or coming in!

You won't want me drifting toward you.
You don't want me going up your nose.
On second thought, you won't have a clue, you
best leave me to just decompose.

REPURPOSED

I just thought of my final wish

and I'm really quite excited about the idea.

I'm not trying to be morbid here,

you tend to think about this stuff

at our time of life,

as our parents age and we talk

about the inevitable,

and it doesn't seem so awful

because we're joking about it

whilst still holding their hand.

Now, if I tell you, you can't rob it.

You've got to think of your own thing.

You can't have someone else's last thing

be your last thing, I think

Be original.

This is your last word as an individual

with a unique pattern of
existence and experience.

Don't be off the shelf,

that's all I'm saying.

(Although having said that,

my sister wants to be carried into the church

to the resounding strains of "Zadok the Priest,"

like, super ostentatious.

I guess I could still pinch it

if I'm lucky enough to go first . . . oh wait!)

Anyway, I want to have a tree planted on me

when I go.

You see, for me it's all about

extending your presence on Earth.

Turn a negative into a positive.

I used to think that I wanted an aspen

because I like the way the leaves move and sound.

Endlessly fluttering,

like a crowd of tiny hands clapping,

creating continuous white noise.

But now I think that could be quite annoying

for those sat under me.

Which, although a pleasing thought,

might not be the best idea.

They might be reminded of my talent for

prattling.

I suspect I'm doing that now.

Anyway, stick me under a tree.

Something fast growing,

and I will nourish it.

I will be in that tree;

that tree will be me.

I will have set aside a sum of money

with instructions for my grandchildren
or great grandchildren

to take that tree, when it is grown,

and go to a PROPER FINE CRAFTSPERSON

(this I cannot stress enough)

A PROPER FINE CRAFTSPERSON

and make a piece of furniture.

Maybe a crib or a carved mantlepiece,

but probably a chair.

Anyway, something very beautiful and useful.

I will be in that chair;

that chair will be me.

I will be a treasured possession.

I will have an afterlife

here on Earth

with my family.

Brilliant.

Unless . . .

They don't go to a
PROPER FINE CRAFTSPERSON

and it's a piece of crap.

Or they make instead

a non-heirloom piece, like

a laptop table or

bunk beds or a TV stand

that, sooner or later,

ends up in the free ads.

Only then can they burn me,

like, ceremoniously,

on a pyre.

And I will enter eternity

and live on . . .

as a media cabinet.

OK, I might have to rethink this.

ARTYFARTY

In the Art Institute today,

I sense that unique gallery atmosphere;

the scent of wealth from immaculate
old Chicago ladies,

low murmurs from a handsome
cosmopolitan couple

in scarves and glasses,

satchelled students,

unsmiling docents.

A cultured ordered space,

intentionally lit,

perfectly regulated,

erudite,

hushed.

I am a middle-aged lady in my best coat today;

looking the part, admiring the art.

But here it should be noted,

I'm feeling incredibly bloated.

Seemingly too spruced to loose
one in the Lautrec,

I feel no one suspects

and a sharp turn on my heel

creates an ambiguous sound on my tour

of the vast parquet floor.

I am a fancy lady in my best coat today,

a smart pop-pop tart, admiring the art.

I'm an Old Master Blaster

roaming haystacks in pasture.

To dispel a little cloud of miasma,

I move under a less popular Monet,

and very gently walk away

so as not to create a vacuum

that follows me across the room.

I am a made-up powdered lady
in my best coat today;

a lipsticked, pointillistic critic.

Less focused on the dappled
visions of impressionism

and more, my dodgy metabolism.

Off to the Romantics and I sit before a storm.

Tossing boats, a wind-whipped sea in oil

that reflects my own inner turmoil.

And for some other lover of Turner,

I leave a little benchwarmer.

I am a metropolitan lady in my best coat today.

A patron of the arts, painting farts

through the halls, exercising prudence

between some major movements.

I exit through the Modern Wing

passing by American Gothic.

I note her frown; her expression is caustic.

He looks ahead, oblivious of her disdain.

And so I wrinkle my nose at the
gentleman beside me

and rather deftly,

place him in the frame.

In the Art Institute today,

I noticed that unique gallery atmosphere;

the scent of wealth from immaculate
old Chicago ladies,

low murmurs from a handsome
cosmopolitan couple

in scarves and glasses,

satchelled students,

unsmiling docents.

A cultured ordered space,

intentionally lit,

perfectly regulated,

erudite,

hushed.

And a little bit smelly.

MEASURED

Apparently, I'm getting shorter,

worn down, past my prime.

Like a pencil daily sharpened,

feeling blunted by bedtime.

One day I will awaken,

find I'm only one inch tall;

a stubby little HB,

almost useless, but not all.

For I will stop and wonder

at the things I wrote and drew

and then feel such contentment at

the marks I left for you.

ACKNOWLEDGEMENTS

Thanks to my husband and daughter for their love and support. Equally, my mother who has been a great motivator, mostly because she kept saying, 'When are you going to finish that bloody book!?' And my sisters and friends that I love so much.

Lizzie Nelson is a British artist currently living in the Chicago suburbs.

If you enjoyed this book, please leave a review.